LEXINGTON PUBLIC LIBRARY

D1116863

RUN,
SEA TURTLE,
RUN

TO MY VERY OWN HATCHLING AND GRANDDAUGHTER,
ESSIE, AND HER WONDROUS JOURNEY —S.R.S.

Text copyright © 2020 by Stephen R. Swinburne
Photographs by Guillaume Feuillet/Naturimages

All rights reserved. International copyright secured. No part of this book may be reproduced, stored in a retrieval system, or transmitted in any form or by any means—electronic, mechanical, photocopying, recording, or otherwise—without the prior written permission of Lerner Publishing Group, Inc., except for the inclusion of brief quotations in an acknowledged review.

Millbrook Press™
An imprint of Lerner Publishing Group, Inc.
241 First Avenue North
Minneapolis, MN 55401 USA

For reading levels and more information, look up this title at www.lernerbooks.com.

Additional images acknowledgments: Minden Pictures/SuperStock, p. 27; Laura Westlund/Independent Picture Service, p. 30.

Main body text set in Stick-A-Round.
Typeface provided by Pintassilgoprints.

Library of Congress Cataloging-in-Publication Data

Names: Swinburne, Stephen R., author. | Feuillet, Guillaume, photographer.
Title: Run, sea turtle, run : a hatchling's journey / by Stephen Swinburne ; photographs by Guillaume Feuillet.
Description: Minneapolis : Millbrook Press, (2020) | Audience: Age 4-9. | Audience: K to Grade 3. | Includes bibliographical references. | Identifiers: LCCN 2019017904 (print) | LCCN 2019020620 (ebook) | ISBN 9781541583801 (eb pdf) | ISBN 9781541578128 (lb : alk. paper)
Subjects: LCSH: Leatherback turtle—Life cycles—Juvenile literature.
Classification: LCC QL666.C546 (ebook) | LCC QL666.C546 S95 2020 (print) | DDC 597.92/89156—dc23

LC record available at https://lccn.loc.gov/2019017904

Manufactured in the United States of America
1-46889-47793-9/9/2019

RUN, SEA TURTLE, RUN

A HATCHLING'S JOURNEY

Stephen R. Swinburne

photographs by Guillaume Feuillet

MILLBROOK PRESS • MINNEAPOLIS

CAN YOU HEAR ME?
SCRITCH, SCRATCH.

I'm a sea turtle.

I'm inside an egg.

My mom built a nest on the beach.
She laid lots of eggs in the nest.
Then she covered us with sand.

~~~~~~~~~~~~~~~~~~~~~

The warm sand kept us safe while we grew.

I peck at the shell with my egg tooth.
CRACK! I hatch.
My brothers and sisters are hatching too.

Let's get out of the nest!
We work together. We are a team.
We are sea turtle hatchlings.

~~~~~~~~~~

I use my long front flippers to climb.
I use my back flippers to help me push.

UP! UP! UP! WE DIG!

We stop and rest.

UP! UP! UP!

We dig and climb higher.

In two days, we reach the top of the nest.

~~~~~~~~~~

We crawl out onto the beach.
We feel the warm sun.

I can see the sky.
I can see the ocean.

~~~~~~~~~~

I am ready to go.

WATCH ME RUN!

I dash. My brothers and sisters dash.
We all dash to the ocean.

Birds soar above us.
Ghost crabs scuttle ahead.
I keep going.
I scoot and scurry.
I leave tracks behind me.

A big stick blocks my way.
I climb over it.

~~~~~~~~~~~~~~~~~~

The ocean is close.
I smell the salty breeze.
I feel the wet sand.

I race faster and faster.
A wave scoops me up.

〜〜〜〜〜〜〜

I wriggle into the sea.
My front flippers flap and beat.
My back flippers steer.

I FLY THROUGH THE OCEAN!
WATCH ME SWIM!

I swim and eat and play.

I will grow bigger each year.

Someday I will come back
to this same beach.
I will lay eggs of my own.

~~~~~~~~~~~~

And one day, my babies
will dash to the ocean.

SEA TURTLE LIFE CYCLE

This book shows the journey of a leatherback sea turtle hatchling as she finds her way to the ocean. Leatherback turtles are one of seven different species of sea turtles. They live in all of the world's oceans.

Adult female turtles leave the ocean and crawl up a sandy beach to lay their eggs. They lay a group of 50 to 120 eggs, called a clutch. About sixty days later, each hatchling breaks through its eggshell with a sharp, bony tip on its face called an egg tooth.

Over a span of two days, the hatchlings work together and dig their way out of the nest. They finish hatching in the morning, evening, or even during the middle of the night. Then the hatchlings make the urgent dash to the sea.

Along the way, they face obstacles such as predators, physical barriers such as rocks and sticks, and the heat of the sun. Only one in a thousand hatchlings survive to adulthood.

Adult turtles can measure up to 6 feet (1.8 m) long and weigh up to 2,000 pounds (907 kg). Female turtles often return to the same beach they hatched on to make their nest and lay eggs for the next generation of leatherback turtles.

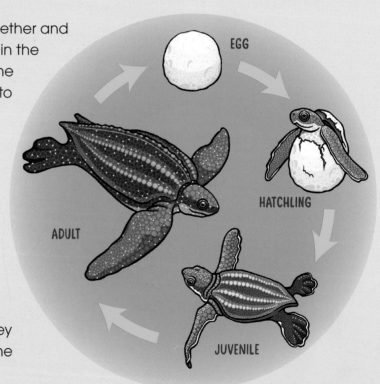

EGG

HATCHLING

JUVENILE

ADULT

HOW YOU CAN HELP SEA TURTLES

1. **Raise money to donate to the sea turtle conservation effort.** Save your allowance, sell sea turtle artwork, or get together with friends to put on a car wash or a bake sale. Donate to an organization that focuses on sea turtle research and habitat protection. Here is a link to get started: https://conserveturtles.org/support-stc-join-stc-and-adopt-a-turtle/.

2. **Use reusable bags and water bottles instead of plastic ones, and don't release balloons.** Trash such as plastic bags and balloons in the water can be mistaken for jellyfish and eaten by sea turtles, causing them harm. Reusable options help keep our oceans plastic free.

3. **Limit the use of pesticides and herbicides in your yard and garden.** Chemicals from these products pollute the waters that sea turtles live in and make ocean animals sick.

4. **Take care of beaches by the ocean.** Participate in a beach cleanup to keep the area free of trash and debris. Knock down sandcastles, and fill in holes when you leave (these can turn into obstacles for hatchlings making their way to the ocean). Put away chairs, umbrellas, toys, and boats when you are done for the day (these can discourage nesting turtles from traveling up the beach).

5. **If you live near an ocean beach, turn off bright lights at night.** Lights confuse hatchlings on their way to the ocean and can make them travel in the wrong direction. Also, extinguish beach bonfires, as these are another source of light.

6. **Don't disturb sea turtle nests, nesting turtles, or hatchlings.** If you want to see a nest, contact a local group or stranding service to attend a watch. A guide will show you how to view the turtles without causing harm. This article offers more tips: https://conserveturtles.org/information-sea-turtles-encounter-sea-turtle/.

SING A SONG ABOUT SEA TURTLE HATCHLINGS

"One in a Thousand" by Stephen Swinburne
https://www.youtube.com/watch?v=Jm00nMZmxgo

FURTHER READING

BOOKS

Cousteau, Phillippe, and Deborah Hopkinson. *Follow the Moon Home: A Tale of One Idea, Twenty Kids and a Hundred Sea Turtles.* Illustrated by Meilo So. San Francisco: Chronicle Books, 2016. In this fiction story, some students help loggerhead turtles find their way to the ocean.

Davies, Nicole. *One Tiny Turtle.* Illustrated by Jane Chapman. Cambridge, MA: Candlewick Books. 2005. Follow the journey of a baby sea turtle in this fictional picture book.

Hall, Kirsten. *Leatherback Turtle: The World's Heaviest Reptile.* New York: Bearport, 2007. Learn cool facts and see photos of leatherback turtles, the world's heaviest known reptile.

Swinburne, Stephen. *Sea Turtle Scientist.* Boston: Houghton Mifflin Harcourt Books for Young Readers, 2015. In this book for older readers, learn about the work of Dr. Kimberly Stewart, a sea turtle scientist and conservationist on the island of Saint Kitts.

Swinburne, Stephen. *Turtle Tide: The Ways of Sea Turtles.* Illustrated by Bruce Hiscock. Honesdale, PA: Boyds Mills, 2010. This illustrated fiction title gives an account of the sea turtle life cycle.

WEBSITES

National Geographic Kids: Leatherback Sea Turtles
https://kids.nationalgeographic.com/animals/leatherback-sea-turtle
Learn facts about sea turtles, see photographs, and more.

Sea Turtle Conservancy: Sea Turtles
https://conserveturtles.org/sea-turtle-conservancy/
Follow this link to find out about sea turtle habitats and track active sea turtles.

Widecast: Caribbean Sea Turtles
http://www.widecast.org/
Learn more about sea turtle conservation.